Peter Kay: The Laughing Legend

Chapter 1: The Early Years

Peter John Kay, a name that has echoed with laughter throughout the United Kingdom and beyond, was born on July 2, 1973, in the charming town of Farnworth, Lancashire, England. From these humble beginnings emerged a comedy giant who would forever change the face of British humor.

Chapter 2: A Comedy Seed Takes Root

Young Peter Kay attended Mount Saint Joseph School, where his early years were marked by artistic inclinations. His father, Michael, an engineer, passed away just before Peter's career in comedy took off, leaving a lasting influence on his life. Peter's mother, Deirdre, an Irish Catholic from County Tyrone, instilled in him the values of faith and perseverance.

Peter's journey to stardom began with a series of odd jobs, including working in a toilet roll factory, a Netto supermarket, and even a bingo hall. Little did he know that these experiences would become comedic goldmines in the future, inspiring episodes of his hit show, "That Peter Kay Thing."

Chapter 3: Education and Transformation

After leaving school with a GCSE in art, Peter embarked on a dramatic shift in his life. He pursued a degree at the University of Liverpool, initially studying Drama, Theatre Studies, and English Literature. However, his heart led him in a different direction, and he switched to a Higher National Diploma (HND) in media performance at the University of Salford's Adelphi Campus School of Media, Music, and Performance. Here, he honed his stand-up skills and found his true calling.

Chapter 4: The Rise of a Comedy Star
Peter's talent was undeniable, and he quickly rose through the ranks of comedy. He won the North West Comedian of the Year award and then, in 1997, triumphed in Channel 4's "So You Think You're Funny" contest. The following year, he earned a Perrier Award nomination for his show at the Edinburgh Fringe Festival.

Chapter 5: Creating Comedy Gold
With his public profile on the ascent, Peter co-wrote and starred in "That Peter Kay Thing" for Channel 4 in 2000. This marked the birth of his iconic character-driven comedy. The success of this series paved the way for "Peter Kay's Phoenix Nights" (2001-2002), a sitcom that captured the hearts of viewers with its hilarious portrayal of a social club run by Brian Potter.

Chapter 6: The Road to Laughter Continues
"Max and Paddy's Road to Nowhere" (2004), a spin-off of "Phoenix Nights," further solidified Peter's status as a comedy genius. He even ventured into the music world, miming to Tony Christie's classic hit "(Is This the Way to) Amarillo," which became a chart-topping sensation in 2005 and raised funds for Comic Relief.

Chapter 7: Master of Parody

In 2008, Peter unleashed his parody prowess with "Britain's Got the Pop Factor... and Possibly a New Celebrity Jesus Christ Soapstar Superstar Strictly on Ice." Under the guise of Geraldine McQueen, he released "The Winner's Song," which climbed to number 2 on the UK singles chart.

Chapter 8: Breaking Records and Winning Hearts
Peter's 2010-2011 stand-up comedy tour made history, earning a place in the Guinness World Records as the most successful tour ever, with over 1.2 million tickets sold. He continued to win accolades, including BAFTA awards for "Peter Kay's Car Share."

Chapter 9: A Comedy Legend's Legacy
In 2016, Peter Kay's BAFTA win for Best Male Comedy Performance marked another milestone in his illustrious career. He also received an honorary doctorate from the University of Salford, a testament to his immense contribution to the entertainment industry.

Chapter 10: Sporadic Appearances and a Triumphant Return

Peter's career had its ups and downs, including a hiatus from 2017 to 2022. However, his triumphant return in 2022 with a new stand-up tour proved that the laughter industry was not complete without him.

Chapter 11: Behind the Laughter
Peek behind the curtain to discover the man behind the laughter. Learn about Peter's personal life, his family, and his enduring commitment to charity work.

Chapter 12: Peter Kay's Enduring Legacy

Peter Kay's legacy is not just in the laughs he's brought to millions but in the way he's touched hearts and transcended comedy. Explore his impact on British culture and the enduring love of his fans.

"Peter Kay: The Laughing Legend" is a journey through the life and career of one of the most beloved comedians of our time. From his humble beginnings in Farnworth to becoming a national treasure, this biography delves into the man behind the laughter and celebrates the enduring legacy of Peter Kay.

Chapter 1: The Early Years

Peter John Kay, a name that has echoed with laughter throughout the United Kingdom and beyond, was born on July 2, 1973, in the charming town of Farnworth, Lancashire, England. From these humble beginnings emerged a comedy giant who would forever change the face of British humor.

Early Life in Farnworth

Peter Kay was born to Michael and Deirdre Kay, into a working-class family in Farnworth. He grew up in a small, close-knit community, and his early years were marked by the warmth of family and a strong sense of community spirit. These formative years in Farnworth would go on to influence his comedy style, which often draws on his experiences of growing up in Northern England.

School Days and the Birth of Comedy

As a student, Peter Kay attended Mount St Joseph School in Farnworth. It was during these school days that he began to display an early flair for comedy. He was known for his quick wit, hilarious impersonations, and his ability to make his classmates and teachers laugh. Little did anyone know that this young boy's talent for humor would eventually catapult him to stardom.

First Steps into Comedy

Peter Kay's journey into the world of comedy began in the local clubs and pubs of Farnworth. He started performing stand-up comedy at various open mic nights, honing his craft and gaining experience in front of live audiences. His observational humor, peppered with references to his upbringing and everyday life, resonated with audiences, and he soon began to build a following.

The University Years

After completing his A-levels, Peter Kay went on to study at the University of Salford. While at university, he continued to perform stand-up comedy and also took an interest in scriptwriting. His experiences at this stage of life would later contribute to his unique comedic perspective and storytelling abilities.

Emergence as a Comedy Star

Peter Kay's big break came when he won the prestigious North West Comedian of the Year competition in 1996. This victory opened doors for him in the comedy world, and he began to perform on a larger scale, appearing in comedy clubs and theaters across the country. His 1998 Edinburgh Festival Fringe show, "The Peter Kay Thing," was a critical success and showcased his distinctive humor.

Television Success

In the early 2000s, Peter Kay transitioned to television, where he achieved immense success with shows like "Phoenix Nights" and "Max and Paddy's Road to Nowhere." His ability to connect with audiences through relatable, down-to-earth humor made him a beloved figure in British comedy.

Conclusion

Peter Kay's journey from the streets of Farnworth to becoming a comedy icon in the UK is a testament to his talent, dedication, and ability to find humor in the everyday experiences of life. His early years in Farnworth laid the foundation for a remarkable career that would bring laughter and joy to millions, cementing his legacy as one of Britain's greatest comedians.

Chapter 2: A Comedy Seed Takes Root

Young Peter Kay attended Mount Saint Joseph School, where his early years were marked by artistic inclinations. His father, Michael, an engineer, passed away just before Peter's career in comedy took off, leaving a lasting influence on his life. Peter's mother, Deirdre, an Irish Catholic from County Tyrone, instilled in him the values of faith and perseverance.

Early Artistic Inclinations

Even during his school days, Peter Kay displayed an early interest in the arts. He was known for his creative talents, including drawing and writing. These artistic inclinations would later find expression in his comedy and scriptwriting, contributing to his unique style.

The Influence of Michael Kay

Peter's father, Michael Kay, played a significant role in his life, even though he passed away before Peter's comedy career blossomed. Michael's influence was profound, instilling in Peter a strong work ethic and a sense of humor that would become a hallmark of his comedic style. Michael's absence left a void in Peter's life, but it also fueled his determination to succeed in the world of comedy.

Deirdre Kay: A Source of Strength

Peter's mother, Deirdre, became a pillar of support during his formative years. Her Irish Catholic background and strong values of faith and perseverance had a lasting impact on Peter. These values would shape his approach to life and comedy, infusing his humor with a sense of warmth and authenticity.

Odd Jobs and Comedy Goldmines

Before achieving fame as a comedian, Peter Kay worked a series of odd jobs to make ends meet. These experiences, including working in a toilet roll factory, a Netto supermarket, and a bingo hall, would later become comedic goldmines. Peter had a keen eye for observing the quirks and idiosyncrasies of everyday life, and these jobs provided him with a wealth of material for his comedy.

"That Peter Kay Thing"

One of Peter Kay's early successes in comedy was the creation of the television series "That Peter Kay Thing." This show, which first aired in 2000, was a collection of standalone episodes, each featuring different characters and scenarios. Many of the episodes drew inspiration from his own life experiences, including his time working in various jobs. The show's down-to-earth humor and relatable characters resonated with audiences, establishing Peter Kay as a rising star in the comedy scene.

Conclusion

Peter Kay's early years were marked by his artistic inclinations, the influence of his father, and the unwavering support of his mother. His experiences in odd jobs provided him with a unique perspective on everyday life, which he would later turn into comedy gold through shows like "That Peter Kay Thing." These formative years laid the groundwork for his future success as one of the UK's most beloved comedians.

Chapter 3: Education and Transformation

Peter's educational path took an unexpected turn when he pursued a degree in Drama, Theatre Studies, and English Literature at the University of Liverpool. His journey eventually led him to a Higher National Diploma (HND) in media performance at the University of Salford, where he developed his stand-up comedy skills. This shift set the stage for his transformation from a student to a budding comedian.

University Years: A Shift in Focus

While many aspiring comedians start their careers with a clear intention to enter the world of comedy, Peter Kay's journey had a different beginning. He initially embarked on an academic path, enrolling at the University of Liverpool to study Drama, Theatre Studies, and English Literature. This choice showcased his interest in the arts and creative expression but did not necessarily point toward a career in comedy.

Exploration at University

During his time at the University of Liverpool, Peter Kay continued to explore his creative side. The university environment provided him with opportunities to delve into the world of drama, theatre, and literature. It was during these formative years that he likely honed his storytelling and performance abilities, skills that would later become central to his comedy.

Transition to Salford and Comedy Development

However, Peter's path took an unexpected turn when he decided to pursue a Higher National Diploma (HND) in media performance at the University of Salford. This decision marked a significant shift in his focus and career trajectory. It was at Salford that he began to develop his stand-up comedy skills, taking the first steps toward a career in the entertainment industry.

The Birth of a Comedian

The move to Salford was a pivotal moment in Peter Kay's life. It was there that he started to refine his comedic style, draw inspiration from his own life experiences, and perform stand-up comedy in local clubs and venues. His transformation from a student studying drama and literature to a budding comedian was underway.

Comedy as a Calling

Peter Kay's decision to transition from academia to comedy was a defining moment in his life. It demonstrated his passion for making people laugh and his willingness to follow his true calling. The skills and experiences he gained during his university years, particularly at the University of Salford, laid the foundation for his future success as a comedian.

Conclusion

Peter Kay's journey through higher education, marked by an initial focus on drama and literature, underwent a transformation as he discovered his passion for comedy. His time at the University of Salford became a critical turning point, where he honed his comedic talents and set the stage for a career that would bring laughter and joy to audiences worldwide. This transition from student to comedian would ultimately shape his legacy as one of Britain's most beloved comedic talents.

Chapter 4: The Rise of a Comedy Star

Peter's undeniable talent quickly propelled him into the spotlight. He achieved notable victories, including winning the North West Comedian of the Year award and a Perrier Award nomination for his show at the Edinburgh Fringe Festival in 1998. His journey into comedy was well underway, and the world was starting to take notice.

North West Comedian of the Year

In 1996, Peter Kay made a significant breakthrough in his comedy career when he won the prestigious North West Comedian of the Year award. This victory was a testament to his comedic prowess and marked his emergence as a rising star in the comedy scene. It was a clear sign that his talent was undeniable and that he was destined for greater success.

Edinburgh Fringe Festival Success

One of the most defining moments in Peter Kay's early career came in 1998 when he performed at the Edinburgh Festival Fringe. His show, titled "The Peter Kay Thing," garnered critical acclaim and earned him a Perrier Award nomination. The Perrier Award, now known as the Edinburgh Comedy Awards, is one of the most prestigious honors in the world of comedy. Peter's nomination solidified his status as a comedian of exceptional talent and originality.

A Growing Following

As Peter Kay's reputation continued to grow, so did his following. Audiences were drawn to his relatable humor, which often revolved around everyday life and the quirks of human behavior. His ability to find humor in the ordinary endeared him to people from all walks of life.

Television Appearances

With his success on the comedy circuit and at the Edinburgh Fringe, Peter Kay began making appearances on television. He showcased his comedic talents on various programs, further expanding his fan base. His natural charisma and down-to-earth charm made him a popular figure on the small screen.

Phoenix Nights and Beyond

One of the crowning achievements of Peter Kay's early career was the creation of the hit television series "Phoenix Nights." Premiering in 2001, the show was co-written by Peter Kay and depicted the eccentric characters and antics of a fictional working men's club. "Phoenix Nights" was a massive success and further solidified Peter Kay's status as a comedy star.

Conclusion

Peter Kay's rapid rise in the world of comedy, marked by victories in prestigious comedy competitions and successful performances at the Edinburgh Fringe Festival, demonstrated his exceptional talent and comedic genius. His ability to connect with audiences through relatable humor and memorable characters set the stage for an illustrious career that would continue to soar to even greater heights in the years to come.

Chapter 5: Creating Comedy Gold

In the year 2000, Peter co-wrote and starred in "That Peter Kay Thing" for Channel 4. This marked the beginning of his iconic character-driven comedy style. The series' success led to the creation of "Peter Kay's Phoenix Nights" (2001-2002), a sitcom that left an indelible mark on British television with its uproarious depiction of a social club run by Brian Potter.

That Peter Kay Thing: A Comedy Gem

In the year 2000, Peter Kay took a significant step in his comedy career when he co-wrote and starred in "That Peter Kay Thing" for Channel 4. This television series marked a turning point in his comedic journey, as it showcased his unique character-driven humor. The show was a collection of standalone episodes, each featuring different characters and scenarios. Drawing inspiration from his own life experiences, including his time working various jobs, Peter Kay created relatable and memorable characters who resonated with audiences.

Phoenix Nights: A Comedy Classic

The success of "That Peter Kay Thing" paved the way for one of Peter Kay's most iconic creations: "Peter Kay's Phoenix Nights." This sitcom, which aired from 2001 to 2002, left an indelible mark on British television. The show revolved around the misadventures of Brian Potter, the eccentric owner of the Phoenix Club, a fictional working men's club.

"Phoenix Nights" was an uproarious comedy that combined slapstick humor, witty one-liners, and unforgettable characters. Peter Kay's portrayal of Brian Potter, a quirky and sometimes downright bizarre club owner, became an instant classic. The series also featured other beloved characters, such as the wheelchair-bound club member Kenny "Dalglish" Senior and the inept bouncer Max. The show's humor was rooted in the eccentricities of its characters and the everyday absurdities of club life.

Cultural Impact

"Phoenix Nights" achieved immense popularity and became a cultural phenomenon in the UK. Its catchphrases, memorable moments, and unforgettable characters entered the national lexicon. The show's success transcended television, inspiring live tours, merchandise, and even charity events.

Legacy of Laughter

The enduring legacy of "Peter Kay's Phoenix Nights" and "That Peter Kay Thing" is a testament to Peter Kay's comedic genius. His ability to create relatable characters and situations, infused with his distinctive Northern English humor, resonated with audiences across the country. These shows not only solidified Peter Kay's status as a comedy superstar but also left an indelible mark on the landscape of British comedy.

Conclusion

The creation and success of "That Peter Kay Thing" and "Peter Kay's Phoenix Nights" were pivotal moments in Peter Kay's career. These shows showcased his exceptional talent for character-driven comedy and cemented his reputation as one of Britain's most beloved comedians. The laughter and joy they brought to audiences continue to be celebrated as part of the rich tapestry of British comedy history.

Chapter 6: The Road to Laughter Continues

The comedy journey didn't stop there. "Max and Paddy's Road to Nowhere" (2004), a spin-off of "Phoenix Nights," showcased Peter's ability to create beloved characters and situations that resonated with audiences. He also ventured into the music world, miming to Tony Christie's classic hit "(Is This the Way to) Amarillo," which became a chart-topping sensation in 2005, raising funds for Comic Relief.

Max and Paddy's Road to Nowhere: A Spin-off Triumph

Following the enormous success of "Peter Kay's Phoenix Nights," Peter Kay and his co-star Paddy McGuinness continued to entertain audiences with their on-screen chemistry. In 2004, they introduced "Max and Paddy's Road to Nowhere," a spin-off series that chronicled the misadventures of the two bouncers, Max and Paddy, as they embarked on a hilarious road trip.

The show retained the same brand of humor that made "Phoenix Nights" a hit, with Max and Paddy's comical antics and unforgettable banter at the forefront. Audiences embraced the spin-off, appreciating the opportunity to further enjoy the beloved characters from the original series.

"(Is This the Way to) Amarillo": Musical Comedy Triumph

Peter Kay's comedic talents extended beyond the realm of television. In 2005, he ventured into the music world with a unique and humorous project that captured the public's imagination. He mimed to Tony Christie's classic hit "(Is This the Way to) Amarillo" for Comic Relief, a British charity telethon.

The accompanying music video featured a star-studded cast, including celebrities and members of the British Armed Forces. Peter Kay, dressed in his trademark style, led a procession of characters in a lighthearted and comical rendition of the song. The video's humor and catchy tune struck a chord with the public, making it an instant sensation.

"(Is This the Way to) Amarillo" not only became a chart-topping hit but also raised significant funds for Comic Relief, showcasing the power of comedy to make a positive impact on charitable causes.

Continued Laughter and Success

These endeavors demonstrated Peter Kay's versatility as a comedian and entertainer. His ability to create beloved characters and situations that resonated with audiences remained a hallmark of his career. Whether on television, in music, or through his charitable work, Peter Kay continued to bring laughter and joy to the lives of countless people.

Conclusion

"Max and Paddy's Road to Nowhere" and "(Is This the Way to) Amarillo" were significant milestones in Peter Kay's career, showcasing his comedic genius and the enduring appeal of his characters. They further solidified his status as a beloved figure in the entertainment world and demonstrated his ability to use humor not only for entertainment but also to make a positive impact on charitable causes. As Peter Kay's road to laughter continued, it was clear that his comedic journey had many more delightful twists and turns ahead.

Chapter 7: Master of Parody

In 2008, Peter Kay's parody skills took center stage with "Britain's Got the Pop Factor... and Possibly a New Celebrity Jesus Christ Soapstar Superstar Strictly on Ice." Under the persona of Geraldine McQueen, he released "The Winner's Song," which soared to number 2 on the UK singles chart, showcasing his versatility as an entertainer.

"Britain's Got the Pop Factor..." - A Hilarious Parody

"Britain's Got the Pop Factor... and Possibly a New Celebrity Jesus Christ Soapstar Superstar Strictly on Ice" was a television mockumentary and parody of talent shows, specifically taking aim at popular shows like "The X Factor" and "Britain's Got Talent." Created and written by Peter Kay, this comedy special was a brilliant send-up of the music and television industry's obsession with manufactured celebrity.

In the show, Peter Kay took on the persona of Geraldine McQueen, a larger-than-life character with dreams of pop stardom. Through a series of hilarious auditions and performances, Geraldine McQueen parodied the clichés and melodrama of reality talent shows, offering a satirical take on the quest for fame.

"The Winner's Song" - Parody Turned Hit

One of the standout moments of "Britain's Got the Pop Factor..." was when Geraldine McQueen performed "The Winner's Song," a tongue-in-cheek, sentimental ballad. The song was a parody of the kind of song often performed by reality show winners, complete with clichéd lyrics and over-the-top emotional delivery.

To the surprise of many, "The Winner's Song" became a massive success in its own right. It resonated with audiences, not only for its humor but also for its catchy tune. The song reached the number 2 spot on the UK singles chart, showcasing Peter Kay's ability to masterfully blend comedy and music.

Versatility as an Entertainer

Peter Kay's success with "The Winner's Song" as Geraldine McQueen highlighted his versatility as an entertainer. He seamlessly transitioned between comedy, music, and parody, demonstrating his ability to connect with audiences across different mediums. This versatility added yet another layer to his already illustrious career.

Conclusion

"Britain's Got the Pop Factor... and Possibly a New Celebrity Jesus Christ Soapstar Superstar Strictly on Ice" and "The Winner's Song" not only showcased Peter Kay's unmatched skills as a parody artist but also solidified his status as a multifaceted entertainer. Through his hilarious take on reality talent shows and his chart-topping parody song, he continued to bring laughter and entertainment to audiences while leaving a lasting mark on the world of comedy and music. Peter Kay's comedic genius knew no bounds, and his ability to master parody was yet another testament to his enduring talent.

Chapter 8: Breaking Records and Winning Hearts

Peter's 2010-2011 stand-up comedy tour made history, securing a place in the Guinness World Records as the most successful tour ever, with over 1.2 million tickets sold. His career continued to flourish, earning BAFTA awards for "Peter Kay's Car Share" and further cementing his status as a comedic genius.

Historic Comedy Tour

In 2010 and 2011, Peter Kay embarked on a monumental stand-up comedy tour that would go down in history. This tour, simply titled "The Tour That Doesn't Tour Tour...Now On Tour," shattered records and made headlines. It secured a place in the Guinness World Records as the most successful comedy tour ever, with over 1.2 million tickets sold.

Peter Kay's ability to connect with audiences through his relatable humor and endearing personality played a significant role in the tour's success. His down-to-earth comedic style resonated with people from all walks of life, leading to sold-out arenas and a comedy tour for the record books.

BAFTA Success with "Peter Kay's Car Share"

While Peter Kay had already achieved tremendous success in stand-up comedy and television, his career continued to flourish in the 2010s. One of his most notable achievements during this period was the creation of "Peter Kay's Car Share," a sitcom that would earn him critical acclaim and further solidify his status as a comedic genius.

"Peter Kay's Car Share" followed the quirky and humorous adventures of two co-workers who share a car ride to work. The show's simple premise and authentic, character-driven humor struck a chord with viewers. Peter Kay's portrayal of John Redmond, a supermarket employee with a penchant for karaoke, and Sian Gibson's portrayal of Kayleigh Kitson, his car-sharing companion, were at the heart of the show's charm.

The series earned several BAFTA awards, including Best Male Comedy Performance for Peter Kay and Best Scripted Comedy, showcasing the show's wide appeal and critical acclaim. "Peter Kay's Car Share" demonstrated Peter's ability to create endearing characters and heartfelt humor.

Cementing a Legacy

Peter Kay's career has been marked by a series of remarkable achievements, from record-breaking comedy tours to award-winning sitcoms. His ability to make people laugh and connect with audiences on a deeply relatable level has endeared him to millions. Peter Kay's legacy as a comedic genius was firmly established, and his contributions to British comedy continued to be celebrated.

Conclusion

The 2010-2011 comedy tour's record-breaking success and the acclaim for "Peter Kay's Car Share" were just two of the many highlights in Peter Kay's illustrious career. His ability to bring joy and laughter to audiences, whether through stand-up comedy, sitcoms, or other creative endeavors, earned him a special place in the hearts of fans and critics alike. Peter Kay's comedic genius had left an indelible mark on the world of entertainment, and his journey of laughter was far from over.

Chapter 8: Breaking Records and Winning Hearts

Peter's 2010-2011 stand-up comedy tour made history, securing a place in the Guinness World Records as the most successful tour ever, with over 1.2 million tickets sold. His career continued to flourish, earning BAFTA awards for "Peter Kay's Car Share" and further cementing his status as a comedic genius.

Record-Breaking Comedy Tour

In 2010 and 2011, Peter Kay embarked on a monumental stand-up comedy tour that etched his name into the annals of entertainment history. This tour, titled "The Tour That Doesn't Tour Tour...Now On Tour," achieved the remarkable feat of becoming the most successful comedy tour ever recorded in the Guinness World Records. With over 1.2 million tickets sold, it was a testament to Peter Kay's immense popularity and his ability to fill arenas with eager fans.

The tour's success was a reflection of Peter Kay's remarkable talent for comedy. His performances were a blend of relatable, observational humor and his unique ability to find humor in the everyday experiences of life. Audiences from all walks of life connected with his down-to-earth style, making the tour a resounding triumph.

BAFTA Triumph with "Peter Kay's Car Share"

While Peter Kay had already left an indelible mark on the world of comedy, his career continued to soar in the 2010s with the creation of "Peter Kay's Car Share." This sitcom, which he co-wrote and starred in, followed the humorous and heartwarming journeys of two colleagues who shared a car ride to work.

"Peter Kay's Car Share" was celebrated for its simple yet effective premise and its endearing characters. Peter Kay's portrayal of John Redmond, a supermarket employee with a penchant for karaoke, resonated with audiences, as did the chemistry between the characters. The show's humor was authentic and character-driven, capturing the everyday humor of ordinary people.

The series received critical acclaim and earned prestigious BAFTA awards, including Best Male Comedy Performance for Peter Kay and Best Scripted Comedy. These accolades underscored the show's appeal and the impact of Peter Kay's comedic genius.

Cementing a Legacy

Peter Kay's career, marked by record-breaking comedy tours and award-winning sitcoms, cemented his legacy as a comedic genius. His ability to connect with audiences on a personal and relatable level, whether through stand-up comedy or television, was a testament to his unique talent.

Conclusion

Peter Kay's 2010-2011 comedy tour's historic success and the acclaim for "Peter Kay's Car Share" were milestones in his illustrious career. They demonstrated not only his ability to make people laugh but also his skill in crafting endearing characters and heartfelt humor. Peter Kay's legacy as a comedic genius was firmly established, and his contributions to British comedy continued to be celebrated, making him a beloved figure in the world of entertainment.

Chapter 9: A Comedy Legend's Legacy

In 2016, Peter Kay's BAFTA win for Best Male Comedy Performance marked another high point in his illustrious career. He also received an honorary doctorate from the University of Salford, recognizing his immense contributions to the entertainment industry.

BAFTA Win: A Continued Triumph

Peter Kay's journey of laughter reached new heights in 2016 when he was awarded the prestigious BAFTA for Best Male Comedy Performance. This accolade was a testament to his enduring comedic talent and his ability to connect with audiences through his memorable characters and hilarious performances. The award further solidified his status as a comedy legend in the UK and beyond.

Honorary Doctorate: A Tribute to His Contributions

In addition to his BAFTA win, Peter Kay received a special honor in 2016 when he was awarded an honorary doctorate from the University of Salford. This recognition celebrated his immense contributions to the entertainment industry and his impact on comedy. The University of Salford, where Peter had pursued his Higher National Diploma (HND) in media performance and honed his stand-up comedy skills, acknowledged his influence on the world of entertainment.

The honorary doctorate was not only a tribute to his comedic genius but also a testament to his journey from a student at the university to a comedy legend. It highlighted the significance of his work in inspiring future generations of entertainers and the enduring legacy he had created.

A Comedy Legend's Legacy

Peter Kay's career, marked by numerous awards, record-breaking tours, iconic television shows, and charitable contributions, leaves behind a legacy that will continue to bring laughter and joy to audiences for generations to come. His ability to find humor in the ordinary, to create endearing characters, and to connect with people from all walks of life has made him a beloved figure in the world of comedy.

Through his work, Peter Kay has not only entertained but also touched the hearts of millions. His legacy extends beyond the laughter he has generated, encompassing his impact on the comedy landscape and his recognition as a true comedy legend.

Conclusion

Peter Kay's BAFTA win and honorary doctorate from the University of Salford were the culmination of a remarkable career that spanned stand-up comedy, television, music, and charity work. These honors celebrated his immense talent, contributions to the entertainment industry, and enduring legacy. Peter Kay will forever be remembered as a comedy legend who brought laughter and happiness to countless lives, leaving an indelible mark on the world of comedy and entertainment.

Chapter 10: Sporadic Appearances and a Triumphant Return

Peter's career had its ups and downs, including a hiatus from 2017 to 2022. However, his triumphant return in 2022 with a new stand-up tour proved that the laughter industry was not complete without him. His comeback was met with overwhelming enthusiasm from fans.

Sporadic Appearances and a Hiatus

After years of consistent success and a string of accomplishments, Peter Kay decided to take a break from the spotlight. Starting in 2017, he reduced his public appearances and put his career on hold for several years. This hiatus left fans wondering when, or if, they would see him back on stage or screen.

Triumphant Return in 2022

In 2022, Peter Kay made a triumphant return to the world of comedy, much to the delight of his fans. He announced a new stand-up tour, signaling his comeback to live performances. This news was met with overwhelming enthusiasm, as audiences eagerly anticipated the return of a beloved comedic talent.

Peter Kay's decision to come back to the stage was a testament to his enduring passion for comedy and his commitment to making people laugh. His comeback tour was a highly anticipated event, and tickets sold out quickly as fans clamored to see their favorite comedian in action once again.

The Laughter Industry Welcomes Him Back

Peter Kay's return to comedy reaffirmed his status as a comedy icon. His ability to connect with audiences and bring joy through humor remained as strong as ever. His sporadic appearances and eventual comeback served as a reminder that the laughter industry was incomplete without his unique brand of comedy.

Conclusion

Peter Kay's career has been marked by highs and lows, but his triumphant return in 2022 demonstrated that his comedic genius is timeless. His ability to make people laugh and brighten their lives through humor has made him a cherished figure in the world of comedy. As he returned to the stage, he continued to inspire laughter and bring happiness to audiences, leaving a lasting legacy in the world of entertainment. Peter Kay's journey of laughter, from his early years in Farnworth to his triumphant comeback, is a testament to the enduring power of comedy to uplift and unite people.

Chapter 11: Behind the Laughter

This chapter delves into the man behind the laughter, offering insights into Peter's personal life, his family, and his enduring commitment to charity work. It unveils the person who has brought joy to millions and highlights the values that drive him.

Family and Personal Life

Beyond the stage and screen, Peter Kay is a family man. He has kept much of his personal life private, but it is known that he is a devoted husband and father. His family provides him with love and support, grounding him in the midst of his busy career. Peter's upbringing in Farnworth, Lancashire, and the values instilled in him by his parents have been instrumental in shaping his character and his approach to life.

Commitment to Charity

Peter Kay's contributions extend beyond entertainment. He is known for his charitable work and philanthropy. One of the most notable examples of this is his involvement in the 2005 charity single "(Is This the Way to) Amarillo," which raised funds for Comic Relief. His willingness to use his comedic talents to support charitable causes demonstrates his commitment to making a positive impact on the world.

Values and Humor

At the core of Peter Kay's comedy is a set of values rooted in everyday life. His ability to find humor in the ordinary and the mundane is a reflection of his down-to-earth personality. His humor is often characterized by warmth, relatability, and a genuine love for people. These values shine through in his comedy and connect with audiences on a personal level.

Legacy of Joy and Laughter

Peter Kay's career has been defined by the joy and laughter he has brought to millions of people. His ability to connect with audiences through humor, his dedication to charitable causes, and his enduring commitment to his craft have solidified his status as a comedic legend. Beyond the laughter, he is a testament to the power of comedy to uplift and unite people, leaving a lasting legacy in the world of entertainment.

Conclusion

Peter Kay's journey, from his early years in Farnworth to his triumphant career in comedy, is a testament to his character, values, and enduring commitment to bringing joy to others. His ability to connect with audiences through humor and his dedication to charitable causes have made him a beloved figure both on and off the stage. As fans continue to cherish his work and his impact on the world of entertainment, Peter Kay remains an enduring source of laughter and inspiration.

Printed in Great Britain
by Amazon

32485865R00030